People Power
Applying Nonviolence Theory

by David H. Albert

foreword by George Willoughby

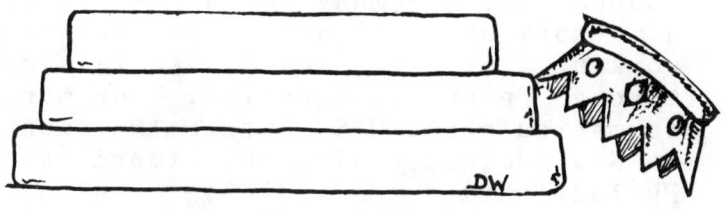

new society publishers

Copyright 1985 by David H. Albert
All Rights Reserved.

Inquiries regarding requests to republish all or part of PEOPLE POWER: APPLYING NONVIOLENCE THEORY should be addressed to:
   New Society Publishers
   4722 Baltimore Avenue
   Philadelphia, PA 19143

ISBN: Hardcover 0-86571-064-3
      Paperback 0-86571-049-X
Printed in the United States of America

Cover design, layout and graphics by David Willoughby and Nina Huizinga.

New Society Publishers is a project of the New Society Educational Foundation and a collective of Movement for a New Society. New Society Educational Foundation is a nonprofit, tax-exempt public foundation. Movement for a New Society is a network of small groups and individuals working for fundamental social change through nonviolent action. For more information about MNS, write: Movement for a New Society, 4722 Baltimore Avenue, Philadelphia, PA 19143. Opinions expressed in this book do not necessarily reflect positions of either the New Society Educational Foundation or Movement for a New Society.

TABLE OF CONTENTS

	PAGE
FOREWORD BY GEORGE WILLOUGHBY	4
DEDICATION	5
PREFACE	6
WHAT IS NONVIOLENT ACTION?	8
NONVIOLENCE THEORY	12
The Sources of Social Power	
Why People Don't Noncooperate With Oppression	
THE CHOICES OF COOPERATING OR NONCOOPERATING AND THEIR RATIONALES	25
THE DYNAMICS OF POWER RELATIONSHIPS	29
HOW IS SUCCESS ACHIEVED THROUGH NONVIOLENT ACTION?	37
THE SOCIAL BAROMETER	46
SOCIETAL MYTHS AND SECRETS	49
SOCIAL FUNCTIONS	52
BUILDING NONVIOLENT ACTION CAMPAIGNS	55
What is Strategy?	
Campaign Strategy	
BIBLIOGRAPHY	60
ABOUT THE AUTHOR	63
RESOURCES FROM NEW SOCIETY PUBLISHERS	64

ILLUSTRATIONS

The Sources of Social Power	16
Blocks to People Noncooperating	20
How Power Works: A Dynamic View	30
The Social Barometer	47

FOREWORD

History tells me that nonviolent struggles have sometimes turned violent. Invariably the explanation follows that "We tried nonviolence, but it didn't work." The real explanation, I suspect, is the failure of those using nonviolence to develop a real understanding of its power when employed by a disciplined, trained people guided by a well-thought-out strategy patiently persisting in the struggle.

For more than thirty years I have studied the theory and practice of nonviolent action, and engaged in many campaigns, testing myself and developing an understanding of this tool of social change. I have traveled to India to study the Gandhian movement which led a successful nonviolent struggle which ended British rule. In the early days of my search, relatively few resources were available for learning the experience of others in nonviolent resistance, but today we have case studies, histories, training manuals, and presentations of theory and strategy.

Two "truths" important to me emerge out of these long years of learning and experimentation. Firstly, ordinary people, you and I, are quite capable of engaging in nonviolent action in defense of our lives, freedom, and humanity. We don't have to be Gandhis or Martin Luther

Kings, nor possess the qualities of a saint. Ordinary people have struggled nonviolently, and their experience can speak to us out of the hidden pages of history.

The second truth is that if ordinary people would employ nonviolence, then it is essential that we discipline ourselves, train ourselves and acquire mastery of nonviolent action. A crucial part of this preparation is an appreciation of the importance, and the study of strategy. **PEOPLE POWER** is an important and helpful contribution. I find it a challenging introduction to the power of nonviolence as a means of effecting social change.

George Willoughby
February 25, 1985

DEDICATION

This book is dedicated to **Krishnamal Jaganathan**, who can answer the most complex and difficult questions about nonviolence with the story of her life.

PREFACE

The aim of this book is to provide activists with a tool to use in their ongoing struggles. It provides a framework for strategizing for social change - whether in the areas of disarmament, women's rights, worker control, environmental safety or whatever - from the perspective of basic nonviolence theory.

In attempting to present a method of applying nonviolence theory, I have consciously set to one side questions about the motivations and ethics behind its use. I do so despite believing that such an exploration is crucial to the very survival of the human race. I believe as did Dr. Martin Luther King, Jr. that in an age of imminent nuclear annihilation, the choices before us as a species are no longer those of "violence or nonviolence", but ultimately "nonviolence or an end to life as we know it."

That this book does not give stronger acknowledgment to the values implicit in nonviolent action in itself suggests a strategy. Activist/writer Dave Dellinger notes that, "The major advances in nonviolence have not come from people who have approached nonviolence as an end in itself, but from persons who were passionately striving to free themselves from social injustice." I believe that the conscious application of nonviolent action techniques by ever-increasing numbers of people makes it more likely that more people will explore the larger moral questions addressed by nonviolence in the future. If you are ready and eager to do so now, don't let me hold you back. (I've put a short reading list at the back for those of you so inclined.)

But for the rest of you who are curious as to how to apply nonviolence theory to your social change work, here goes....

WHAT IS NONVIOLENT ACTION?

Before asking what nonviolence theory is, we must describe the field of activity it attempts to explain. That is, "nonviolent action".

Nonviolent action comprises a group of techniques and strategies by which groups of people can wield their social power effectively. It generally occurs in conflict situations in which a group of people decides to go outside normal "socially validated" channels in order to effect changes in what they believe to be unjust, oppressive or exploitative situations.

Descriptions of nonviolent action usually display the motivations or purposes of the people doing the describing. The four most common descriptions are not exclusive of each other. Taken together, they give us a good picture of the breadth of nonviolent action.

1. A means of resolving conflict and effecting reconciliation: This view of

nonviolent action is very common, especially among those committed to it from a religious perspective, such as Quakers or Christian pacifists. It implies that the major work of nonviolent activists is the search for the best possible outcome for all parties to a conflict.

2. **A technique for waging conflict efficiently, with as little damage as possible to the human person and effecting the fullest development of the human personality:** This description of nonviolent action is essentially that of Mohandas Gandhi, the leader of the nonviolent struggle for the liberation of India from British rule. Gandhi recognized the critical importance of being ready and willing to wage conflict in the service of justice, even at great personal sacrifice. The waging of conflict through the practice of what he called **satyagraha** ("truth-force" or "truth-grasping") is not something to be avoided, but can and should be a growing experience for all involved. We must be aware, however, that this description will not provide a simple moral formula for evaluating at what point particular tactics or strategies cross over the line between any abstract notions of nonviolence and violence. Gandhi believed that these conceptions could only take on meaning for the individual in the substance of his/her individual situation which would provide the raw material for the striving after truth.

3. **A method of wielding social, political and economic power:** Democratic and especially anarchist theories often view nonviolent action as the norm rather than the exception. For the sake of efficiency and the meeting of larger numbers of social needs, people constantly delegate power and authority to others within the society. Conflict occurs when competing groups within the society attempt to have this power wielded in the service of their own interests. Nonviolent action then becomes a normal part of the political process of conflict by which these competing interests and needs are balanced. This 'pluralist' theory of power, however, often fails to account clearly for the fact that people are often unconscious of the control they actually have over their social and political institutions. Hence, nonviolent action can also be seen as....

4. **A way in which people discover their social power:** If it is true that people often unconsciously delegate their own power within a society, then nonviolent action is a process by which people rediscover and then mobilize their forgotten social power. In his book Why We Can't Wait, Martin Luther King, Jr. stresses over and over again that the commitment to and use of nonviolent action gave Black Americans a sense of their own dignity and moral worth for the first time which they could not possibly have achieved had the goals of the Civil Rights movement been sought through other

means. The Civil Rights movement exposed social myths about racism in the United States, and gave Black Americans an understanding of their own power, a power which in fact had always been there, waiting to be tapped.

It is clear from the foregoing descriptions that nonviolence theory encompasses a field of activity which is much broader than those actions clearly labeled as "nonviolent" by their practitioners. This is not surprising, as the term "nonviolence" doesn't even appear in the dictionary until 1929. As a means of struggle, the term "nonviolence" first appears in print in Clarence Marsh Case's **Nonviolent Coercion: A Study in Methods of Social Pressure** in 1923. While some understanding of the dynamics of nonviolent struggle dates back at least as far as Aristophanes' **Lysistrata** - a Greek play of the fifth century B.C. in which women unite in refusing to sleep with their husbands as long as the men insist on going to war - the theory of nonviolent action and its recognition as a unified system of thought is just more than a half century old.

NONVIOLENCE THEORY

Nonviolence theory is a **theory of power** based on one single principle: **ALL POWER - PERSONAL, INSTITUTIONAL, SOCIAL, POLITICAL OR ECONOMIC - DEPENDS ULTIMATELY UPON THE OBEDIENCE, CONSENT AND/OR COOPERATION OF THOSE OVER WHOM THE POWER IS WIELDED.** This theory remains valid despite the fact that those who wield power often resort to violence in order to keep it.

Simply speaking, power is the capacity of human beings to organize or manipulate their environment (including other human beings, their thoughts, motivations, needs and desires, as well as their creations and artifacts) for human ends. In all major world ideologies and religions, power is seen as neither a positive nor a negative concept. From ancient Judaism to contemporary Christianity, from nineteenth century Marxism to modern feminism, power is conceived of as simply a fact of existence. Power is not considered to be either good or evil.* However, while neutral in itself, power can be used for either good or evil ends. It can be dispersed and/or shared among large numbers of people in the course of their human relationships, or concentrated in a small handful of people or powerful institutions. Power is never destroyed; it is constantly transferred and shared among people and institutions, as people always need to organize their environments in order to survive. It can be thought of as "power over" when concentrated in the hands of the few, or as

---

*The single exception is the Indian religion Jainism. According to Jain religious ideology human beings must atone for the very act of living - because living, and the organization of the environment which goes with it, necessarily causes suffering to other living beings - human, animal or plant - equally entitled to go about their own spiritual searches. Traditionally, Jains at the end of their lives become rigorously ascetic hermits and quite literally starve themselves to death in penance for their use of power during their earthly existences. This ideology heavily influenced Gandhi, who sought a method of wielding social power with as little damage to others as possible and which would aid them in their own spiritual search.

"power with" or "power among" when shared widely, but as power it still exists.

When we think about nonviolence theory, we are usually examining **social power**. Social power is the capacity to organize or control, directly or indirectly, the behavior of others through purposeful human action. What is special about nonviolent action is that it attempts to **cut off the sources** of an opponent's power in a conflict situation, rather than combatting the final **product** of these sources, as in organized violent strategies. In a war situation, for example, those employing nonviolent strategies do not attempt to directly combat an opponent's military strength, but attempt to cut off the opponent's ability to use or maintain a military force - by sapping the sources of military supply, readiness, and personpower, and political support and cooperation. Because it deals with sources of power rather than the final product, nonviolent action strategies are thus often more **efficient** - in cases where nonviolent overthrows of oppressive governments have been effected (El Salvador and Guatemala in 1944; Iran and Bolivia in 1979), they have succeeded only after less efficient strategies have failed. And those who choose to wage conflict nonviolently, rather than adopting it as a result of tactical considerations, are also more likely to consider how those same strategies, growing out of the same theory of change, can be used to build a better society.

The Sources of Social Power

If social power ultimately comes from those over whom the power is wielded, then we need to know what forms these sources of power take in order to limit their availability to an opponent through nonviolent action. Gene Sharp, in his monumental pioneering study **The Politics of Nonviolent Action**, catalogs seven sources of social power, which can, as already noted, be used for good or ill. The social power of a person or institution rests upon the ability to mobilize these sources to achieve their ends:

1. **Authority** - the perceived right and voluntary acceptance of command and obedience without sanctions.

2. **Human resources** - the number, proportion, and organization of people who obey, cooperate, or provide special assistance to the wielder of power.

3. **Skill and knowledge** - the quality of human resources at the disposal of the wielder of power can often be as important a source of power as the quantity of such resources.

4. **Material resources** - control over property, economics, means of communication and transportation.

SOURCES OF SOCIAL POWER

5. **Ideological factors** - the ability to manipulate the beliefs of others based on a common faith or mission. Nationalism, patriotism, or religious beliefs are all examples of ideological factors which deeply affect the extent and intensity of a government's power.

6. **Psychological factors** - the charisma of the wielder of power and people's habits and attitudes toward obedience and submission. Corporations, for example, have long known the value of childhood education in instilling submissive behavior in future workers, whose submission can then be transferred from the classroom to the workplace.

7. **Sanctions** - the methods of enforcement of obedience available to a wielder of power. Sanctions are essentially the bottom line as a source of power. Democratic theorists have often pointed out that the concealing of sanctions (especially overtly violent ones) away from public awareness is critical in maintaining democracy. Thus the sanctions can only be relied upon in crisis situations.

It should be noted that the very ability to impose social sanctions derives from the obedience and cooperation of at least some subjects. For example, the obedience of military personnel is needed to put down a rebellion. Sanctions are thus themselves dependent on the wielder of power's ability to draw on **other** sources of power. Furthermore, sanctions may be effective and fiercely brutal in certain situations, but the need to rely on them may in fact be a sign of the breakdown of other significant power relationships.

Nonviolent action is not magic. An effective activist must analyze carefully the sources of an opponent's power so as to be able to strategize effectively in cutting them off. The degree to which these sources are limited is the degree to which the institution's or person's power is limited; when these sources of power are cut off, a new social relationship, a new arrangement of social power, comes to be.

Why People Don't Noncooperate with Oppression

Much has been written about why people enter into cooperative social relations with each other. The reasons are often varied and complex and can be examined from many different theoretical perspectives too numerous to address here. Most of them ultimately add up to the same thing: people think (sometimes mistakenly) that they benefit psychologically, socially, economically, or even metaphysically from such cooperation.

The relatively simple question which nonviolent strategists must address is why people **don't noncooperate** with uses of power which oppress or exploit them. Gene Sharp in **The Politics of Nonviolent Action** states that there are at least seven **blocks** preventing people from noncooperating. By removing these blocks, the power of nonviolent action is mobilized:

1. **Habit** - People are used to cooperating even though they have not completely thought out why they do so. Generally speaking, the fact that people cooperate from habit is a good thing, as an atmosphere of trust makes society significantly more efficient and less conflict-

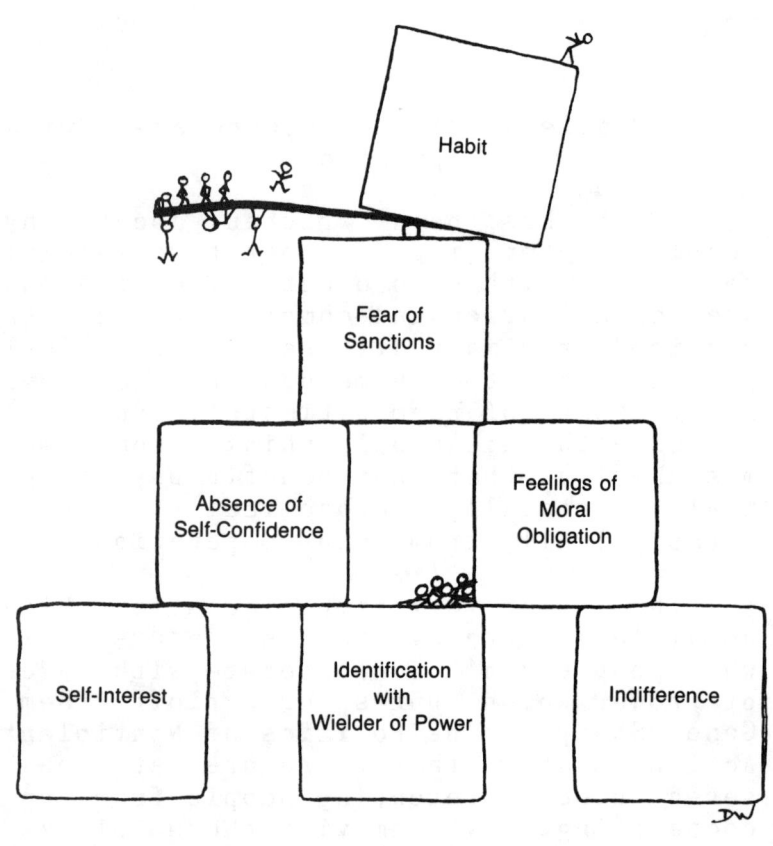

BLOCKS TO PEOPLE NONCOOPERATING

riddled. It should also remain clear, however, that habitual and unthinking cooperation can provide the groundwork for the abuse of power.

2. **Fear of sanctions** – People don't noncooperate because they fear the stated consequences of doing so. As we noted earlier, these sanctions remain real only because **some** people continue to agree to enforce them.

3. **Absence of self-confidence** – Gandhi called absence of self-confidence "the habit of fear," and thought of it as the single most significant block to nonviolent action and to the building of a truly free, democratic and caring nonviolent society. People fail to noncooperate with oppression because they lack sufficient confidence in themselves, their judgment, and their capacities for resistance. Lack of self-confidence is reinforced by dozens of social mechanisms, especially in capitalist, patriarchal and/or bureaucratic societies or those under colonial or imperialist control. The use of random, unorganized, "non-strategic" violence can often result when people realize their own oppressed condition, but lack the self-confidence or the will to noncooperate with it in an organized fashion. Hence they may act out of desperation, rather than as a result of clear thinking.

4. **Feelings of moral obligation** – People don't noncooperate because, as a result

of customs, mores, and beliefs they have learned, they feel an "inner compulsion" to cooperate, submit, or obey. Four kinds of beliefs lead to this feeling of moral obligation not to noncooperate:

>A. Belief in the "common good of society" - People learn early in their lives that to noncooperate is "anti-social", with expected consequences worse than the injustice they are experiencing or asked to acquiesce to or participate in.
>
>B. Belief in the "suprahuman" qualities of ruling institutions or persons - People believe that certain persons or institutions command obedience and submission as a result of qualities above and beyond human control. Examples include "divine right of kings," the "natural superiority of men over women", "manifest destiny," God having entrusted the State with control over temporal affairs, "white man's burden" (as an excuse for imperialism), and "predetermination" or "predestination" as the cause of people's class or caste positions. To challenge such people or institutions, even when they act unjustly, is often viewed as also challenging one's obligations to an even higher authority.
>
>C. Belief in the legitimacy of command - People will often submit to those in positions of authority

because they feel morally obliged to uphold the social order, even if they disagree with the individual obligations placed upon them or feel that the common good is not being served by their submission. A good example is the well-known fact that air force pilots may obey commands which they personally disagree with, such as dropping bombs on innocent civilians in war, but would never kill innocent people at home.

D. Belief in the justice of commands - People actively obey commands when they conform to what they believe to be right anyway.

5. **Self-interest** - People may refuse to noncooperate either to advance their own interest or position, or to avoid inconvenience or trouble for themselves. This is especially true of agents of oppressive institutions who may not favor the institutions' oppressive policies, but stand to lose social and economic position by refusing to cooperate with them. Many interesting case studies have been done of prisoners who gain status and position by helping to maintain their own jails.

6. **Identification with the wielder of power** - People may not noncooperate because they have a "need to belong" and identify with those who have power. Civil servants, even when poorly treated by the institutions for which they work, none-

theless may continue to carry out their functions because they identify with the very institution which exploits them. More extreme are the cases of slaves identifying with and rejoicing in the good fortunes of their masters.

7. **Indifference** – People often cooperate, though not enthusiastically, because they are willing to tolerate the rule of those exercising power.

THE CHOICES OF COOPERATING OR NONCOOPERATING AND THEIR RATIONALES

Both cooperation and noncooperation **always** involve a choice. This is true even when one of the choices is likely to lead to great hardship, suffering, or even death. But for those who cooperate with the oppression of others or do not resist their own oppression, admitting even to themselves that they have made a choice would constitute a blow to their own self-respect and esteem, almost surely to be accompanied initially by confusion or deep anger, which may be acted out in violence. Clinical psychologist Marshall Rosenberg in his book **From Now On: A Model for Nonviolent Persuasion** (St. Louis: Community Psychological Consultants, 1969) has noted nine different ways of thinking or habitual "rationales" which people use, consciously or unconsciously, to obscure for themselves or for others the possibility of choice:

1. Directly denying that choice exists. ("I did what was necessary; there weren't any alternatives.")

2. Attributing the cause of action or inaction to the actions of others. ("I arrested him because he refused to move.")

3. Attributing the cause of action or inaction to vague, impersonal forces. (God's will, the immutable forces of history, etc.)

4. Attributing the cause of action or inaction to one's psychological history, condition, or personal habits. ("My parents taught me never to rock the boat.")

5. Attributing the cause of action or inaction to those in authority. ("I just do what I'm told.")

6. Attributing the cause of action or inaction to group pressures. ("Everyone else went along; they made me do it.")

7. Attributing the cause of action or inaction to institutional policies, rules or regulations. ("I don't like the fact that they use my tax money to kill people, but it's the law and I have to pay it.")

8. Attributing the cause of action or inaction to gender, social, or age roles. ("Children are to be seen but not heard; who am I to question my elders?")

9. Attributing the cause of action or inaction to uncontrollable impulses or

tendencies. ("I'd like to do something, but I'm dreadfully afraid; I guess I'll never change.")

To which we can add a tenth: attributing the cause of action or inaction to the cynical and/or despairing view that it doesn't make any difference what one does. ("It doesn't matter; things won't change anyhow.")

A nonviolent activist must carefully examine what rationales people utilize to obscure the reality that choices are open to them, and must find ways to convince them that life-affirming changes in their social, political or economic environments can only come about through recognizing and exercising the possibilities of choice.

It must be stressed again that nonviolent action is not magic. In social struggle, nonviolent action is the **art** of, firstly, limiting the opponent's sources of power, and secondly, removing the blocks people have to noncooperating with oppressive use of power. As in any art, nonviolent activists learn through experience and by carefully studying the experience of others. By examining an opponent's sources of power, by analyzing the blocks which keep people from actively resisting injustice, and by acting in a disciplined and determined, though loving, manner, activists can find in nonviolent action the foundations upon which to build a new society.

Even in describing social power from a static perspective, we should remain aware that the actual perspective is much more complex. The oppressed virtually always have some sources of power which they can and do mobilize, even if minimally. Similarly, there are almost always blocks or limits to the extent to which an oppressive person or institution can utilize power. These can also be analyzed in terms of the general schema presented above so that the oppressed's sources of power can be enhanced, and the blocks on oppressive uses of power made stronger. Recognizing the complexity of each individual social situation cannot but assist in enriching our insights into the workings of nonviolent action.

THE DYNAMICS OF POWER RELATIONSHIPS

The forms which the sources of power take are the same in all social relations. But the nonviolent activist is deeply aware that power itself is a dynamic social relation. As the sources of power are depleted or cut off, the extent and intensity of a person's or institution's power itself diminishes; as the sources are replenished, so the extent and intensity of power grows. Power is always shifting; even in oppressive situations which may on the surface look static, human beings, and human institutions, are in a constant process of transformation.

The diagram on the following pages, adapted again from the work of Gene Sharp in **The Politics of Nonviolent Action**, illustrates this dynamic process:

HOW POWER WORKS

A NONVIOLENT ACTIVIST PERSPECTIVE

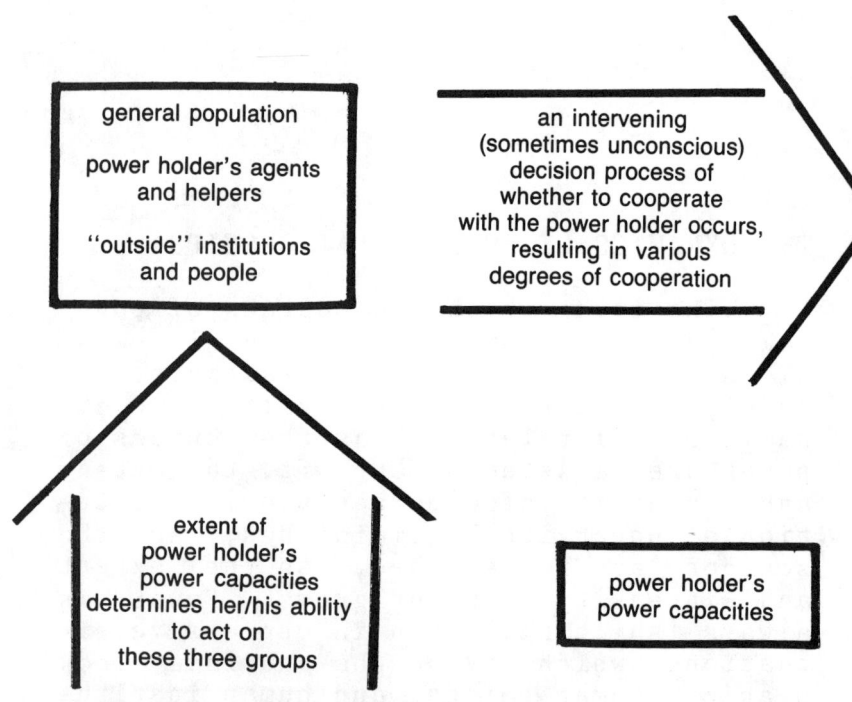

Adapted from Gene Sharp, *The Politics of Nonviolent Action,* Chapter One. Boston, MA: Porter Sargent, 1973

degree of cooperation/
resistance from
general population,
including the oppressed

degree of cooperation/
resistance from
power holder's agents

degree of cooperation/
resistance from
"outside" institutions
and people

degree of cooperation/
resistance to
power holder
from these three groups
determines availability
of sources of power

extent, quality and availability
of these sources
increases, maintains,
reduces or abolishes
power holder's
power capacities

authority
human resources
skills and knowledge
ideological factors
psychological factors
material resources
sanctions

This continual process increases or decreases a power holder's power capacities. This process ends only when that power is disintegrated.

Graphically illustrating this dynamic of power are the events of the final stages of the Iranian Revolution in 1978-1979, where an oppressed and virtually unarmed people overthrew the most vicious and brutally repressive dictatorship in the Middle East backed by the U.S. government, the most powerful military power in the history of the world. By using this example, we are not attempting to judge the present Iranian regime either positively or negatively. To do so fairly would require placing contemporary Iranian society within the context of Islamic culture, the political situations of the countries surrounding Iran, and the pressures of the two superpowers fighting for control of the area's resources, in addition to a detailed analysis of the events following the revolution. But the Iranian struggle is particularly instructive because its leadership had no ideological commitment to nonviolence. Nor did they have a social vision which would be shared by most people who "believe" in nonviolence as a philosophy. On the contrary, the Iranian example singularly demonstrates that the theory of nonviolent action can explain the shifting dynamics of social power regardless of the belief systems or social goals of those involved, and regardless of our agreement or disagreement with their politics.

The former Shah, even as late as January 1978, had substantial access to all seven sources of power. He possessed the traditional authority accorded an Iranian monarch: a huge army, secret police and bureaucracy were at his disposal; a full complement of highly skilled government officials and U.S. advisors; control over the huge Iranian national treasury, oil fields, radio and television stations; strong Iranian nationalism, symbolized by the person of the Shah himself; entrenched habits of obedience and submission to a ruler's authority; and access to the full range of sanctions, legal and military, as well as the expectation on the part of his opponents that they would be subject to arrest, torture or death for their opposition. During the course of the final year of struggle, some 40-60,000 unarmed demonstrators would be killed. The blocks to noncooperation would thus also have seemed overwhelming; the vast majority of Iranians were virtually silent in the realm of political affairs for almost twenty five years.

From January until September 1978, increasing numbers of people demonstrated against the Shah's oppressive regime. People were killed at each of the demonstrations, and a set period of mourning (40 days) would take place until the next demonstration, thus creating a climate of rising tension. On September 7th, martial law was declared in Iran's major cities in an attempt to prevent the next series of demonstrations. But on September 8th, hundreds of thousands of people, having overcome their "habits of fear," refused to stay in their homes; more than 3,000 were gunned down on the streets of Tehran, Iran's capital city. Following that day's events, even after President Carter telephoned the Shah from Camp David to offer his "full support", power relationships in Iran changed radically. Workers in Iran's 20 billion dollar a year oil industry called a series of general strikes and refused to bend to pressure and appeals to their "moral obligation" to return to work. Inspired by the success of the oil workers' resistance, general strikes spread among the population, bringing the economy to a standstill. Recognizing the people's overwhelming opposition to the Shah, the military, questioning its own obligations, began to show signs of insubordination in refusing to repress the population. Finally, even the U.S. government, the most important "outside" institution, having originally attempted to back the Shah and protect its own investments by sending riot control weapons and even emergency oil shipments, changed in its perceived "self-interest" to maintaining its stake under a new regime, and advised the Shah to leave the country.

We see then that within the course of a year, the power capacity of the former Shah, which he had built up over twenty-six years, was almost entirely dissipated. The intense resistance to his rule, coupled with an increasing lack of cooperation on the part of the government's agents and outside institutions, eroded his sources of power: his authority was seriously undermined; his access to resources and information was severely limited; his status as a symbol of Iranian nationalism was destroyed; the people's awareness of and faith in their own powers of resistance were strengthened; and the Shah's ability to apply sanctions was curtailed. It was only a matter of time before his power would entirely disintegrate, resulting in his being overthrown.

The Iranian Revolution illustrates the dynamics of nonviolent action particularly well because, in contrast to Gandhi's struggle for Indian Independence, it happened so quickly, and without any ideological commitment to nonviolence. At no time before attaining power in February 1979 did Ayatollah Khomeini, the chief strategist and leader of the struggle, or other Islamic leaders of the revolt call for or utilize armed struggle against the former Shah, his agents, or the armed forces. This is not because they were pacifists, but because they understood only too well that their power clearly did not flow, as Mao quite incorrectly maintained about "all power", from the barrel of a gun. The understandably deep resentment, as well as continuing and well-founded fears, felt by the people of Iran after a long history of oppression, both internal and external, surely played a role in the development of punitive forms in the new arrangement of power, and can jeopardize the development of a nonviolent value system. Nonetheless, we should not be distracted from the chief lesson it has to teach us. A virtually unarmed people, having experienced twenty-six years of dictatorship, systematic repression, and torture, with its would-be leader two thousand miles away (Khomeini was in exile for sixteen years prior to 1979), overthrew the most powerful, technologically sophisticated and inhumanly brutal regime in the Middle East, backed by the greatest military power in the history of the world, **through nonviolent action.***

---

*For a much fuller account of this struggle, consult **Tell the American People: Perspectives on the Iranian Revolution**, edited by David H. Albert, available from New Society Publishers, $6.45 postpaid.

HOW IS SUCCESS ACHIEVED THROUGH NONVIOLENT ACTION?

George Lakey, in his essay "Sociological Mechanisms of Nonviolence: How It Works," notes that success is achieved in a campaign employing nonviolent action in one of three ways:

1. **Nonviolent coercion** – The opponent's power capacities are limited to such an extent that the ability to maintain the status quo is taken away. An interesting historical example of nonviolent coercion was the government bureaucracy's resistance to the Kapp regime in Germany in 1920. After a right-wing coup d'etat against the Weimar Republic, the entire corps of civil servants within the government refused to cooperate. Checks couldn't be signed or cashed; letters went untyped. Within three days, the regime collapsed.

Another more recent example is the last phase of the Iranian Revolution. In January 1979, the Shah, with the active consultation of the United States, attempted to appoint Shapur Bakhtiar, formerly an opposition leader, to lead a new government and to appease the population. But the vast majority of people refused to recognize Bakhtiar's authority and wanted the Shah removed; significant elements in both the military and civilian arms of government simply disregarded his orders, resulting in his downfall.

2. **Accommodation** - Accommodation is the most common method by which success is achieved through nonviolent action. Opponents give in, not because they have changed their minds or because they are powerless, but because the changed social situation brought about by nonviolent action now confronts them with a possible condition which may be still more unsatisfactory. A good example of this was the willingness of white Atlanta businessmen to accede to the demands of the Civil Rights movement for integrated business facilities because sit-ins and demonstrations had resulted in declining business during the Christmas season. The business community did not have to accede to the demands, but the possibility of the continuing spectacle of demonstrations meant a further loss to Atlanta's business and tourist trade as well as a blow to prestige through the moral stigma of being known as a "racist" city.

A less well-publicized case of accommodation as a partial result of nonviolent action marked the end of the Viet

Nam War. While popular opposition to the War in the United States may have limited the full extent of U.S. involvement, so that, for example, nuclear weapons were never used, opposition by itself was never able to alter significantly the face of public policy. And at no time were the insurgents, backed by the North Vietnamese, ever able to successfully challenge the full might of American military forces. But toward the end of the War, a substantial and increasing number of U.S. soldiers began "search and avoid" missions, expressing through their "nonviolent actions" an unwillingness to continue to prosecute the War, whatever government policy might actually be. Faced with the growing demoralization of the Armed Forces and thus increasing inability to gain military objectives through the use of troops, and unwilling to take the more drastic steps which would have been necessary to get the troops to fight effectively, the Government accommodated itself to the changed situation by pulling troops out of combat areas and trying to fight the war almost totally from the air, finally resulting three years later in the downfall of the U.S.-supported Saigon regime.

Still another example of accommodation is the current complete though unofficial moratorium on orders for new nuclear power plants in the United States. Utility companies and the nuclear industry will never admit that nuclear power opponents have prevented them from ordering new plants or have persuaded them of the rightness of the anti-nuclear cause. Nevertheless, the crescendo of anti-nuclear activism in the United States, occurring almost always in the form of nonviolent action and virtually entirely outside the electoral process, has so undermined business confidence in nuclear power investment, the electric consumer's trust of the public utilities and of the regulatory process, and the people's confidence in nuclear safety that the industry has clearly **accommodated** itself to a future without plans for new nuclear plants. This is despite continuing U.S. government support for nuclear power and despite government projection in the early '70s of more than four hundred operating nuclear power plants in the U.S. by the year 1990, two thousand by the year 2000. This "about-face" essentially occurred all within a five-year period (1975-1980), representing a spectacular success for nonviolent action gained in the face of opposition by some of the most powerful capitalist forces in the world. It is one of the very few times in human history that people's power has stopped technological "innovations" favored by business interests in their tracks. That the struggle to prevent the building of nuclear power plants ordered at an earlier date and to eliminate all nuclear power plants and weapons still goes on should not blind us to our past successes, and to an understanding of the process of accommodation by which it occurred.

3. **Nonviolent conversion or persuasion** – Through conversion, the opponent has inwardly changed. Persuasion of an opponent in the course of social struggle is the least well-understood and perhaps most important method of success in thinking about how conflict should be waged in a nonviolent society.

It is important to remember that persuasion is a crucial element in almost all social struggles, violent or nonviolent. It happens as a part of the normal interplay of social and political forces. The Russian Revolution of 1917 was made possible by the desertion of the Czar's soldiers; government analyst Daniel Ellsberg's release of the Pentagon Papers after being converted to oppose the Viet Nam War played an important role in galvanizing support for an end to the War. More recently, we have experienced several cases of former nuclear engineers and scientists quitting their jobs and joining anti-nuclear struggles in the U.S. and Canada, and cases of Israeli soldiers refusing to serve in occupied territories on the West Bank.

But the act of persuasion is not usually so dramatic. While there are cases, such as that of the Indian King Ashoka (4th century B.C.) giving up martial conquest and embracing Buddhism and nonviolence as a way of life, more often the act of persuasion slowly changes the balance of social forces. Nonviolent activists must keep this in mind. Often social and institutional change may appear slow, much slower than the rate of change in public opinion. Other times it may be quick and sudden, but usually there is a long and unappreciated process of change which takes place before this comes about.

Attempts at nonviolent persuasion can have useful though unintended consequences of great significance which go unrecognized by activists themselves, who may see their work as having essentially failed. In the mid-1950s, the pacifist Fellowship of Reconciliation, learning of famine in the Chinese mainland, launched a "Feed Thine Enemy" campaign. Members and friends mailed thousands of little bags of rice to the White House with a tag quoting the Bible, "If thine enemy hunger, feed him." As far as anyone knew for more than ten years, the campaign was an abject failure. The President did not acknowledge receipt of the bags publicly; certainly no rice was ever sent to China.

What nonviolent activists only learned a decade later was that the campaign played a significant, perhaps even determining role in preventing nuclear war. Twice while the campaign was on, President Eisenhower met with the Joint Chiefs of Staff to consider U.S. options in the conflict with China over two islands, Quemoy and Matsu. The generals twice recommended the use of nuclear weapons. President Eisenhower each time turned to his aide and asked how many little bags of rice had come in. When told they numbered in the tens of thousands, Eisenhower told the generals that as long as so many Americans were expressing active interest in having the U.S. feed the Chinese, he certainly wasn't going to consider using nuclear weapons against them.

In the course of a lifetime in pursuit of radical social change through nonviolent action, Mohandas Gandhi isolated eight factors in the control of activists which make conversion more likely. As conversion of "fence-sitters", even if not of the main opponent, is virtually always a necessity, even in aiding a course of nonviolent coercion, these suggestions are worth at least evaluating against our own experience:

1. Refraining from violence or hostility.

2. Real attempts to gain the opponent's trust.

3. Refraining from humiliating the opponent - this includes **not** relying on numbers alone to produce "victory", (it may produce stubbornness and bitterness instead), but rather relying on the power of the truth which you hold.

4. Making visible sacrifices for one's cause - you may be asking your opponent to sacrifice what s/he sees as her/his own self-interest or self-esteem; to convince them, you should be prepared to

do the same.

5. Carrying on constructive work - positive activity reduces the negative image that a society may have of those who noncooperate.

6. Maintaining personal contact with the opponent - insures maximum possible mutual understanding.

7. Demonstrating trust of the opponent - when you have high expectations of an opponent, these expectations may encourage her/him to live up to them.

8. Developing empathy, good will, and patience toward the opponent - why address yourself to an opponent at all unless you assume s/he can change? If you deeply understand the motives, expectations, attitudes and perceived interests of opponents **as people**, your actions are likely to become more powerful.

It is in attitudes toward the main opponent that nonviolent actions may differ from each other. While persuasion plays a role in all nonviolent action, indifference toward persuasion of the main opponent, often as an understandable result of a long history of oppression, bodes ill for the kind of situation which may result after a new arrangement of power has come to be. Thus while the tactical uses of nonviolent action, such as that used in the Iranian Revolution, may be more effective than violence in uniting a large majority of people in achieving specific goals, it will not necessarily result in new power relations which are more just than those they succeed. The spirit in which any struggle, violent or nonviolent, is carried out, will always remain an important factor in determining the values inherent in the new power relationships.

THE SOCIAL BAROMETER

We have seen earlier that power is a dynamic social relation. We have also noted that there is a whole range of actors in any social conflict, with various points of view and different roles to be filled. By enlarging our framework for strategic thinking by considering all the actors in a social conflict, rather than just the main opponent, we are in a better position to evaluate potential nonviolent tactics and strategies.

One way to visualize this framework is to construct a "social barometer":

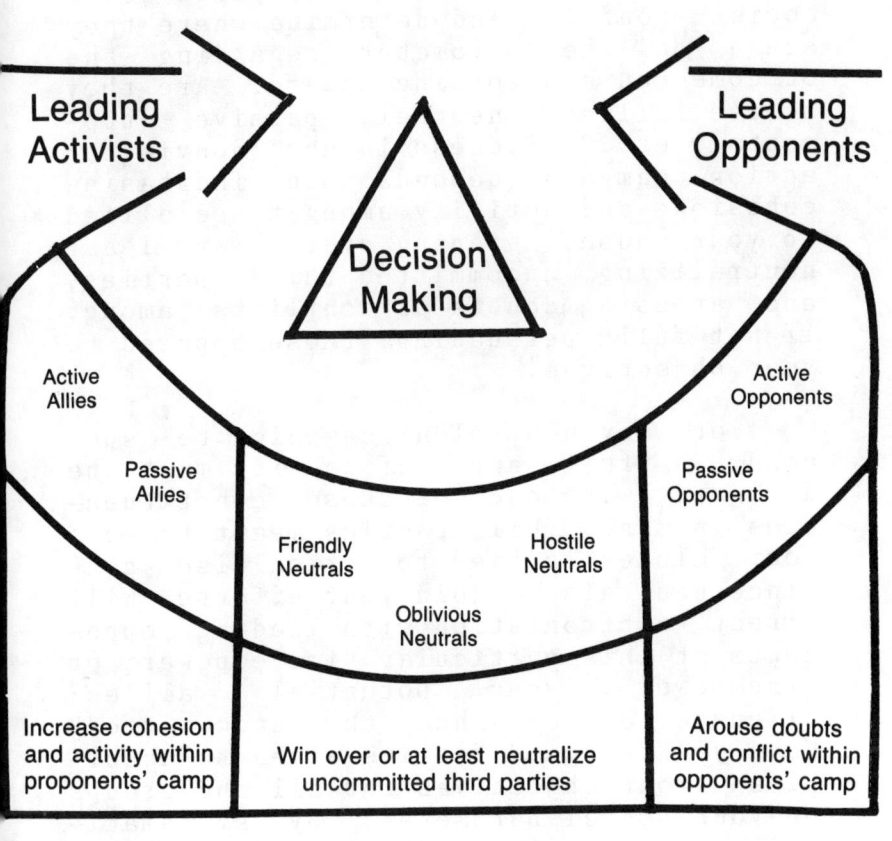

Tasks for Activists

Social Barometer

List all the potential parties to a social conflict and determine where they stand on the barometer regarding the outcome you are working toward. Are they active allies, neutral, passive opponents, etc.? Success in any nonviolent action campaign depends upon increasing cohesion and activity among those allied to your cause, winning over or at least neutralizing uncommitted third parties, and arousing doubts or conflicts among, if not fully persuading, those opposed to your objectives.

For any nonviolent campaign to succeed, a full array of tactics must be designed with each of these constituencies in mind. Will tactics meant to move your closest allies to action also convince neutrals to join your efforts? Will direct confrontation with leading opponents at this particular time empower or disempower your potential allies? alienate or convince the uncommitted? Have you designed tactics aimed to accomplish your objectives for **all** the groups on your social barometer? By systematically considering each of your proposed nonviolent action tactics according to their potential effects upon the social barometer, and by consciously evaluating them this way afterwards, your strategic thinking, and your campaign, is almost sure to become more effective.

SOCIETAL MYTHS AND SECRETS

Earlier we noted that among the main blocks to noncooperation are people's feelings of moral obligation toward those who in fact oppress or exploit them. For an exploitative system to function effectively over the long term, it must be kept secret that people's obedience and/or cooperation is responsible for creating unjust or life-denying conditions for some or for many. To keep these secrets or to prevent their unmasking these secrets, as sociologist Max Weber has pointed out, social systems develop a public set of beliefs, values and ideologies called **societal myths** which we are socialized to believe or to want to believe. Examples might range from belief in the "natural superiority of men" to the United States guaranteeing "liberty and justice for all" despite its long and continuing history of racial injustice and exploitation, to the use of the expression "free world" to stand for nations such as Chile, South Africa, Guatemala, El Salvador, Pakistan, and the Philippines, some of the harshest antidemocratic regimes in the world, to building still more nuclear weapons in the belief that they actually constitute a "defense against nuclear attack".

It is useful for the nonviolent activist to know that a planned tactical approach toward the exposing of **societal myths** as being only myths can play a crucial role in arousing people to action. Twentieth century thinkers and historians such as Hannah Arendt have repeatedly pointed out that people are often more upset and more likely to be driven to action by the unveiling of hypocrisy than by the prevailing conditions of injustice which hypocrisy seeks to hide. Given an already well-thought-out action strategy, the conscious isolation and exposure of **societal myths** can act as a very powerful catalyst in moving people toward nonviolent social struggle.

One graphic illustration should suffice. In Boulder, Colorado in 1982, civil defense authorities unveiled their plans for crisis relocation in case of nuclear attack. Anti-nuclear activists seized this opportunity to expose the social secret that there is no such thing as a defense against nuclear attack. Public hearings discredited the plan as utterly unworkable, destroying the myth that government officials could be entrusted with matters of safety in case of grave national emergency. With this myth destroyed, increasingly large numbers of citizens in Boulder have turned to questioning basic U.S. military "defense" posture, and the nuclear terrorism which it requires. While many may have eventually come to question what they were being told anyway, activists in the area have no doubt that revealing the myth of "crisis relocation" for what it was greatly accelerated that process.

SOCIAL FUNCTIONS

In India, social reformers have arisen generation after generation for centuries in opposition to the caste system. Despite the fact that the vast majority of the population suffered under the injustices perpetrated by the system, and that a very large proportion of the population at any one time would have agreed that the system was unjust, most of the social reformers failed. The reason for this is that, however unjust the operation of caste as a social institution, most people saw it as functioning to fulfill a set of social needs which they perceived would not be fulfilled in other ways. The caste system guaranteed one a position in the social hierarchy, a traditional occupation, a series of marital norms which made the arranging of marriages easier, a social welfare system which guaranteed that each particular caste grouping would take care of its own poor, aged, and sick members, and a fluid religious system of rewards and punishments in the "cosmic hierarchy" which made the world seem both understandable and just. Given the functions fulfilled by the caste system, it is no wonder that most people would not overthrow an admittedly unjust system in favor of an unknown one.

In the few cases where reformers were successful, they were able to offer tangible alternative models for meeting most of these needs in other ways, without the oppressive "side effects". As a result, reformers were generally far more successful when they operated outside the confines of traditional Hinduism in offering new social and religious systems (such as Buddhism, Sikhism, Islam, and Christianity) to fulfill needed functions, than when they sought caste reform from within. And today, the caste system is rapidly breaking down, not so much from the pressure of social reformers, but because the system is failing to perform the social functions it formerly fulfilled, as a result of the pressure of increasingly harsh economic conditions.

A more contemporary example is the unwillingness of most Americans to abandon reliance on military and nuclear defense. Many Americans can see the evils and dangers inherent in current defense strategies - the huge costs to the economy, the dangers of nuclear war, etc. Yet, they also perceive a need to defend the territorial integrity of the United States, the traditional freedoms of speech, assembly, press, and religion, their homes and their families. They are willing to accept the "by-products" of current military defense strategies because they don't perceive a way in which these needs will be fulfilled by other, less costly and oppressive, means. Arms talks, nuclear freezes, "build-downs", etc., while perhaps constructive, offer no alternatives in the meeting of these needs, and hence do little or nothing to shake most Americans' reliance on the traditional means of defense. Only by offering the real possibilities of performing what are perceived as socially necessary defense functions will anti-military activists likely make inroads into broad American support for military spending and nuclear defenses.

Before conducting campaigns, nonviolent activists should carefully analyze the social institutions or activities they will be opposing. They should understand what social functions claimed for the institutions are really "societal myths" and devise strategies for exposing them as such. But they should also understand what social functions are really performed by these institutions, however oppressive they are in their actual operation, and ensure that they have ways of making the public aware of how these functions can be performed, by other institutions or activities, or by reforming existing institutions.

BUILDING NONVIOLENT ACTION CAMPAIGNS

What is Strategy?

A strategy is a broad plan or outline which combines separate actions in such a way so as to achieve sought-after objectives. It is the product of a coherent social analysis and of a realistic vision. It develops a theory of change into an action program that can suggest immediate action projects, as well as long-range perspectives which will carry a group through years of hard work, setbacks, and short-term successes.

A strategy must be dynamic, taking account of changes in social relations which take place during the course of a campaign. It is a tool, not a dogma. Hence a strategy should:

-- provide a long-range framework for short-term actions;

-- provide a framework for considering what results are likely to follow from proposed tactics;

-- enable us to find tactics consistent with basic goals;

-- help us make decisions about the use of people's energies, resources, and skills;

-- provide a framework for action which can be continually evaluated and modified by experience;

-- help increase understanding of the relationship between the goals of a particular campaign and other issues;

-- suggest creative ways for people to live, work and relate to each other supportive of their basic goals;

-- help resolve tensions between personal lifestyle and/or workstyle and continual involvement in social and political struggle.

Good strategy is like an accurate road map. It will lead you to a predetermined goal, but it will not determine the goal for you. Success achieved through good strategic thinking can and often has demoralized activists when they have discovered all too late that their choice of goals was unsatisfying. But poor strategy or lack of strategy, even with well-defined goals and a large degree of support, can be even worse. Like following the wrong road map, it can mean expending more and more time, energy and resources without getting any closer to your goals.

Campaign Strategy

Only **after** your goals are well-defined, after you are clear that your goals require a nonviolent action campaign rather than some other form of activity (such as building alternative institutions), and after you are clear what **minimal** demands need to be met in order for you to consider your campaign successful, are you ready to strategize. Using the materials presented in this pamphlet may be one of many ways to evaluate your campaign strategies. Use the following list of questions throughout he campaign to clarify your own and your group's or organization's strategic thinking:

1. What institutions, people and ideologies stand in the way of your achieving your goals?

-- What specifically are the sources of their social power?

-- Are there actions or directions which might be taken which could limit these sources of power more effectively?

-- Do any of your actions limit some of these sources of power but have the side effect of increasing others? which ones?

-- If your strategy is successful, what shifts in power dynamics will be realized in obtaining your demands?

2. Who are your potential allies?

-- Do the allies you specifically aim at mobilizing have enough potential power to effect the changes you seek?

-- What specific "blocks" stand in the way of your potential allies withholding cooperation from your opponents? What rationales are your potential allies now relying on to prevent their own increasing commitment to your cause?

-- How will your planned campaign overcome these blocks?

-- Are there actions or directions which might be taken which could remove these blocks more effectively?

-- Do any of your actions remove some of these blocks but have the side effect of increasing others? which ones?

-- What societal myths does the campaign expose? Will their exposure be sufficiently clear to motivate people to engage in nonviolent struggle?

-- What real social functions are currently performed by the institutions or activities you are opposing? How will you project how these social functions can be performed by other institutions or activities, or by reforming the institutions you oppose, in less oppressive ways?

-- If your strategy is successful, what kind of shift in power dynamics will be realized in obtaining your demands?

Strategy is an art. Like all arts, doing it well requires an effective combination of practice and study. We urge all those interested in building a just, peaceful and humane community and world order to become artists in the field of nonviolent action!

BIBLIOGRAPHY

The following books are recommended for those especially interested in nonviolent action from a strategic perspective:

Joan Bondurant, **Conquest of Violence**, revised edition, (Berkeley, CA: University of California Press, 1965)
Robert Cooney & Helen Michalowski, **The Power of the People: Active Nonviolence in the United States** (Culver City, CA: Peace Press, 1979; revised and updated edition forthcoming from New Society Publishers in 1986)
Dave Dellinger, **More Power than We Know** (Garden City, NY: Anchor Press/Doubleday, 1975)
Susanne Gowan, George Lakey, William Moyer, & Richard Taylor, **Moving Toward a New Society** (Philadelphia, PA: New Society Press, 1976)
Richard Gregg, **The Power of Nonviolence** (revised edition - New York: Schocken, 1966)
George Lakey, **Strategy for a Living Revolution** (San Francisco: W.H. Freeman, 1973; revised edition forthcoming from New Society Publishers, 1987)
Joanna Rogers Macy, **Despair and Personal Power in the Nuclear Age** (Philadelphia, PA: New Society Publishers, 1983)
Brian Martin, **Uprooting War** (London: Freedom Press, 1984)
Gene Sharp, **The Politics of Nonviolent Action** (Boston, MA: Porter-Sargent, 1973)

Gene Sharp, **Social Power and Political Freedom** (Boston, MA: Porter-Sargent, 1980)

The following books are recommended for those especially interested in nonviolent action from a moral or ethical perspective:

Hannah Arendt, **On Violence** (New York: Harcourt-Brace, 1970)
Barbara Deming, **We are All Part of One Another: A Barbara Deming Reader**, edited by Jane Meyerding (Philadelphia, PA: New Society Publishers, 1984)
Mohandas Gandhi, **My Experiments With Truth** (Boston, MA: Beacon Press, 1957)
Mohandas Gandhi, **Nonviolent Resistance** (New York: Schocken, 1961)
Paul Goodman, ed., **Seeds of Liberation** (New York: George Braziller 1964), especially Albert Camus, "Neither Victims Nor Executioners"
Philip Hallie, **Lest Innocent Blood Be Shed: The Story of the Village of Le Chambon and How Goodness Happened There** (New York: Harper & Row, 1980)
Martin Luther King, Jr., **Why We Can't Wait** (New York: Harper & Row, 1964), especially "Letter from a Birmingham Jail"
Pam McAllister, ed., **Reweaving the Web of Life: Feminism and Nonviolence** (Philadelphia, PA: New Society Publishers, 1982)

Thomas Merton, **A Nonviolent Alternative** (New York: Farrar, Straus & Giroux, 1980)

A.J. Muste, **The Essays of A. J. Muste**, edited by Nat Hentoff (Indianapolis, IN: Bobbs-Merrill, 1967), especially "On Holy Disobedience"

Henry David Thoreau, **Walden and On Civil Disobedience** (Boston, MA: Houghton-Mifflin, 1960)

Leo Tolstoy, **The Kingdom of God is Within You** (Lincoln, NE: Univ. of Nebraska Press, 1984)

Leo Tolstoy, **On Civil Disobedience and Nonviolence** (New York: Bergman, 1967)

Leo Tolstoy, **Resurrection** (New York: Signet, 1966)

Lanza del Vasto, **Return to the Source** (New York: Schocken, 1972)

ABOUT THE AUTHOR

David H. Albert is a member of New Society Publishers. Philadelphia, PA. He was the North American representative to the Asian Seminar on Nonviolent Direct Action in India, 1978-1979, and has worked with nonviolent action and community groups in India, Sri Lanka, and Thailand. He also serves as Media Relations Director of the Fellowship Commission in Philadelphia, a human rights agency, as a board member of the New Society Educational Foundation and the A. J. Muste Memorial Institute, and as Board Chairman of the Pennsylvania Council to Abolish the Penalty of Death. He was editor of the book **Tell the American People: Perspectives on the Iranian Revolution** (1980) and the tabloid **Why Nonviolence? Nonviolence Theory and Application for the Nuclear Age** (1978, 1983).

RESOURCES FROM NEW SOCIETY PUBLISHERS

We Are All Part of One Another: A Barbara Deming Reader edited by Jane Meyerding; foreword by Barbara Smith. Essays, speeches, letters, stories, poems by America's foremost writer on issues of women and peace, feminism and nonviolence spanning four decades. 320 pages. 1984. Paperback $10.95; Hardcover $24.95.

Reweaving the Web of Life: Feminism and Nonviolence edited by Pam McAllister. Essays, songs, interviews, speeches, short stories, photographs. Annotated bibliography. Index. 448 pages. 1982. Paperback $10.95; Hardcover $19.95.

Nonviolent Struggle in the Middle East by R. Scott Kennedy & Mubarak Awad. Two activists - one Palestinian, one American, explore nonviolent strategies. 40 pages. Photographs. 1985. $2.95.

To Order
Send check to:
    New Society Publishers
    4722 Baltimore Avenue
    Philadelphia, PA 19143

For Shipping: Add $1.50 for first publication, 40 cents each additional.

Ask for our complete list.